Original title:

Island Rhythm

Copyright © 2025 Creative Arts Management OÜ
All rights reserved.

Author: Julian Montgomery
ISBN HARDBACK: 978-1-80581-705-5
ISBN PAPERBACK: 978-1-80581-232-6
ISBN EBOOK: 978-1-80581-705-5

Drifting with the Moonlit Flow

Under a sky where the palm trees sway,
Napping seals join in a midnight play.
Silly crabs do their jitterbug dance,
While a lost flip-flop takes its chance.

The stars are bright, winking with glee,
As fish throw a party, wild and free.
Laughter echoes from the waves so bold,
Even the seaweed can't help but fold.

Tranquil Shores and Twilight Melodies

On the beach where the seagulls squawk,
Shells gather round for a gossip talk.
Turtles wearing hats lounge in the sun,
As beach balls tumble, oh, what fun!

Crabs in tuxedos strut with pride,
While starfish dance on the outgoing tide.
The ocean hums a quirky tune,
While jellyfish groove 'neath the glowing moon.

The Pulse of Paradise

In this land where the coconuts fall,
The piña coladas beckon with a call.
Bananas play ukuleles so sweet,
While the sand tickles our wiggly feet.

Mangoes swirl in a fruity ballet,
As parrots laugh in a colorful way.
Here, every wave is a tickling tease,
And laughter floats on the warm sea breeze.

Chasing Shadows on Sandy Shores

Beneath the sun, where shadows chase,
A penguin in shades picks up the pace.
With each silly step, the seagulls cheer,
While turtles wonder, "What's the fuss here?"

Footprints dance along the golden sand,
As starfish tag along, hand in hand.
The horizon giggles, plays hide and seek,
While we all join in, feeling quite chic.

The Whispering Secrets of the Sea

The fish are gossiping, oh so sly,
They giggle and wiggle as boats pass by.
A crab in a tux, all dressed to impress,
Flirts with a seashell, what a funny mess.

Seagulls squawk tales that make no sense,
While dolphins play tag—what a fun pretense.
The waves carry whispers in bubbles of air,
As sunbathers dance, without a single care.

Windswept Waltz of the Skies

The kites are soaring, playing tag with clouds,
While breezes hum tunes that attract big crowds.
A parrot with jokes takes center stage,
Cracking up everyone from a leafy cage.

The breeze does a shuffle, gives hats a lift,
Giggling at sunburns is its favorite gift.
Under blue canopies, laughter does swirl,
As skies turn cheeky in this windy twirl.

The Lull of the Lapping Tide

The shore sings softly, with waves that tease,
Tickling the toes of those on their knees.
A starfish does yoga, stretching out wide,
While a turtle watches, full of sea pride.

Each splash brings giggles, they dance and sway,
A conch shell's snore makes the crabs run away.
The shore's gentle lull makes everyone grin,
As little fish swim like they're dancing a spin.

Murmurs Through the Mangroves

The roots are all twisted, a jungle of fun,
Where monkeys trade secrets under the sun.
A flamingo slips, loses its cool, you see,
It flaps and then wobbles—oh, what a spree!

The owls are rapping in a rhythmic beat,
While lizards show off with their fancy feet.
A whispering breeze makes branches applaud,
In this silly giggle, they all feel like gods.

Serenade of the Solstice Sun

The sun did dance upon the shore,
With wiggles and giggles, it begs for more.
The crabs in tuxedos, prancing around,
Tapping their claws to a jolly sound.

Seagulls audition for a comical show,
Flapping their wings like they're putting on flow.
They dive and they swoop, with laughter so bright,
While fish play hide and seek, pure delight!

Echoes Beneath the Coconut Canopy

Beneath the palm trees, whispers abound,
A monkey named Larry jumps up from the ground.
He swings and he sways on a leafy vine,
Making funny faces while sipping his wine.

The breeze plays a tune, so wacky, so clear,
As the toucans gossip, oh, lend me your ear!
They gossip and cackle, shaking their heads,
While sleeping iguanas dream of soft beds.

Dance of the Distant Horizon

The dusk spills colors, a wild parade,
As dolphins show off, a splashy charade.
They flip and they flounder, in synchronized glee,
Inviting the stars for a wacky spree.

The moon's wearing shades, striking a pose,
While jellyfish jive, in bright disco clothes.
They float and they shimmer, with laughter so grand,
Creating a rave where the ocean meets sand!

Melody of the Gentle Breeze

The breeze tickles flowers, causing them to laugh,
While ants form a conga line, each with a staff.
They twirl and they spin, a parade in the grass,
As the butterflies join, with flair and sass.

A prancing gecko wears a tiny hat,
He struts with great pride, like a top acrobat.
The ticks and the tocks of this wild serenade,
Make nature's laughter a fabulous charade!

Sanctuary of Solitude

In a hammock that's swaying, I take a quick nap,
Dreaming of fish that might fit in my cap.
With a parrot that's squawking some questionable jokes,
And a crab that has dancing moves like a bloke.

Sunburned and grinning, I sip on my drink,
While the seagulls are plotting to steal from my sink.
They chat in the wind with their comical caws,
As I flip through my book of fish stories and flaws.

Heartbeat of the Sunlit Sands

Beneath the hot sun, the sand starts to giggle,
Each grain seems to wiggle and twist like a wiggle.
I'm buried in laughter, or maybe just sand,
With seashells that sing as they come to my hand.

A crab waltzes past me, he's dressed in a vest,
He offers me jokes and I think he's the best.
With a twist and a turn, then a sidestep or two,
We break into laughter, just me and my crew.

Whispers of the Palm Fronds

The palms are all gossiping, swaying with glee,
Spilling their secrets as they dance with the breeze.
I join in their chatter, my face in a grin,
While coconuts laugh at the weak kneed spin.

A dog in the shade is snoring away,
Dreaming of chasing the sun all day.
His tail starts to wag like a drum on the beat,
As if he's off chasing some ants for a treat.

Serenade of the Distant Horizon

The horizon's like velvet, it winks in the light,
And fish in their fins seem to dance through the night.
Playing a tune that makes waves start to sway,
While I join the chorus, "Come on, let's play!"

A sailor's old parrot is squawking a song,
Of treasure and pirates, oh how they belong!
With a swish and a splash, while mermaids all cheer,
I can't help but chuckle and give a loud cheer!

Salted Breeze and Glistening Dreams

A seagull stole my sandwich, oh my!
It waddled away, that crafty guy.
The sun's so bright, I squint and grin,
While chasing my lunch as it leaps to win.

The sand's too hot, I dance like crazy,
In flip-flops flapping, feeling quite lazy.
A crab tiptoes, a sideways glance,
I join its shuffle, a clumsy dance.

The salty air tickles my nose,
As I search for treasures beneath the clothes.
A bottle pops, fizzing like cheer,
Turns out it's just a seaweed beer.

So let's laugh and play with gleeful cheer,
In this sunny place, we have no fear.
With every wave, a chuckle will soar,
As we bask in the jokes of the ocean floor.

Adventures in the Shaded Cove

In the cove where shadows play,
I found a crab named Bob, hooray!
He wore a hat, quite tall and proud,
Claiming the title of King aloud.

With my friend, we built a grand sand fort,
But soon the tide turned, oh what sport!
The walls collapsed with a squishy sound,
Bob waved his claws, defending his ground.

We searched for shells with voices too,
Each one sang a tune or two.
The jellyfish danced in a wobbly line,
Requesting a concert, quite divine!

As evening fell, we shared our thrill,
With shadows stretching, so we could chill.
Laughter echoed, the stars aglow,
In the cove, where the funny things flow.

The Cadence of Crashing Waves

The waves dance high, quick and spry,
Making the beach a lullaby.
A surfer fell, and lo! What grace,
He flopped like a fish, a right-faced chase.

Shells roll in with the ebbing tide,
Each one hiding a giggle inside.
I found a starfish, grumpy and slow,
Claiming he's too cool for this show.

The squawking gulls join in the fray,
Making demands for snacks every day.
A snackless hour? Oh, what a plight!
These feathered foes cause a funny fight.

The sun dips low, as laughter fades,
In the cadence of waves, our joy cascades.
For every splash, a silly tale,
As we ride the rhythm, light and pale.

Whirlwinds of Whispering Waters

In whirlwinds sweet, the waters swirl,
Fish play hide and seek, oh what a whirl!
With fins aflutter, they tease my toes,
Turning the sea into laughter's prose.

A dolphin flips, so light and spry,
I swear it winked, as I passed by.
With each wave crashing on the shore,
I find more reasons to laugh and explore.

The wind tickles my cheek like a friend,
Making the long day seem to blend.
As I sip coconut from a funky straw,
A wave sneezes, with a laugh and a paw!

So here's to whirlwinds and watery fun,
With giggles and splashings under the sun.
Each joke a ripple, in the sea's embrace,
In this funny world, we've found our place.

Reflections on the Waterscape

Splashing around, a fish takes a dive,
Twirling like dancers, they seem so alive.
The seaweed waltzes, a green little sprout,
While crabs practice salsa, there's no shadow of doubt.

Seagulls are gossiping, sharing their tales,
Since when did they join in the lunch hour gales?
The sun waves goodbye in a sunset parade,
As flip-flops go flying, it's a comical charade.

The Cadence of Celestial Shores

On the shore, sandcastles rise with pride,
Till a wave shows up, and they all just hide.
With bucket and spade, kids dig with glee,
But seagulls will swoop for a snack of their spree.

Under bright umbrellas, the folks start to snooze,
While jellyfish ballet stairs go comically askew.
A beach ball bounces, it springs with a laugh,
As sunscreen becomes a slippery giraffe.

Nocturnal Ballad of the Seafoam

Moonlight giggles upon the calm waves,
As seafoam gathers, mischief it braves.
Starfish are twinkling, give a wink in the night,
While crabs dance the shuffle, in quite a delight.

Coconuts roll in the dim evening glow,
While hermit crabs complain, 'It's too much to tow!'
The night air is filled with giggles and sighs,
As dolphins swap stories under starry skies.

Harmonies of the Waves' Embrace

Waves play the drums, with laughter they crash,
While a conch shell echoes an offbeat splash.
Flip-flops are lost in a rhythmic ballet,
As beach towels tango at the end of the day.

Children are giggling, chasing their dreams,
While a wayward crab plots its grand schemes.
The sunset bows down, giving night a high-five,
As all join the chorus, feeling so alive.

Tidal Echoes of Distant Shores

Waves arrive with a splash and a giggle,
The seagulls squawk in a comical wiggle.
Flipping burgers, forgetting the brine,
Sunburns from laughter, oh, how they shine.

Flip-flops flying, they land on the sand,
Dancing in circles, what a silly band.
Splashing in puddles, oh what a sight,
Everyone chuckles, into the night.

The breeze carries stories of laughter galore,
Sandy-haired kids, forever wanting more.
Jellyfish are laughing, they wiggle with glee,
While umbrellas dance like they're wild and free.

As the tide pulls back with a cheeky grin,
Fishing for fun, where do we begin?
The shells are like treasures, a pirate's delight,
With treasure maps drawn in the soft moonlight.

Dreams Beneath the Azure Aegis

Beneath the blue sky, dreams twist and swirl,
Sandy toes do the cha-cha, oh what a whirl!
Coconuts falling, they bounce with a thud,
While sunbathers giggle, they're stuck in the mud.

Palms sway to whispers, a laugh in the breeze,
Crabs moonwalk sideways, oh how they tease!
Pineapple hats on our heads, what a sight,
The day drifts on with a comical light.

Sipping on smoothies while laughing aloud,
As jellyfish float by, they really feel proud.
The sandcastles tumble, a dramatic fall,
While the tide claps its hands, we're having a ball!

As stars twinkle down, lighting up the shore,
We dance with wild joy, wanting nothing more.
Waves lapping gently, a giggling refrain,
Under the moon, we forget all the pain.

The Saga of Seaside Sojourns

Seagulls are squabbling for chips on the pier,
While grandpa's asleep with a can full of beer.
Sandwiches fly, oh what a bold move,
The tide plays a melody, come feel the groove!

We dig up the treasures, shells filled with glee,
While laughter erupts like a sweet jubilee.
Mom's chasing crabs, what a spectacular sight,
While dad builds a fortress, not one wall is right.

Between splashes and giggles, we race with the tide,
Jumping over waves, our spirits won't hide.
Fish gossip quietly, all under the blue,
While we trade our secrets, a silly crew.

As sunset paints laughter across the vast bay,
We dream of tomorrows in our playful way.
With stars as our audience, we bow with a cheer,
These are our moments, forever held dear.

Melodic Metronome of the Ocean

Ocean hums softly, a rhythmic delight,
Shells tap dance around, in the soft evening light.
Turtles in sunglasses stroll casually by,
While dolphins play tag with a flip and a fly.

Picnics of laughter, on checkered cloth laid,
A sandwich escapes, that little rascal's made.
The waves tap their feet to a jubilant song,
All the beachgoers join in, laughter prolonged.

Seashell collectors with pails in their grip,
Stumble and fumble; oh, it's quite the trip!
The tide pulls away like it's up to some game,
While pelicans strut in a funny parade.

As day turns to dusk, a dance of sweet fate,
We sway to the rhythm, it's never too late.
Hand in hand we frolic, joy woven in air,
Underneath the full moon, without any care.

Ocean's Poetic Embrace

The crab danced sideways with flair,
While seagulls squawked without a care.
A fish wore sunglasses, looking cool,
Winking at folks in the swimming pool.

The jellyfish jived in jelly shoes,
While starfish played their favorite blues.
Conch shells chimed like a phone that's lost,
In this beach party, we're never tossed!

When sandcastles topple, it's a blast,
The surfboard rode like a rocket fast.
A beach ball bounced in a hilarious spree,
Laughing and giggling, oh can't you see?

So join the laughter, let spirits soar,
You'll find the ocean's forever door.
With frolicsome waves and a joyous crowd,
Embrace each moment, sing it loud!

Windswept Verses

A sailor's hat flew, a comical sight,
Chasing a gull in the afternoon light.
The wind whispered jokes as it tangled my hair,
Creating a symphony of breezy despair.

The parrots squawked out punchlines in glee,
As I laughed with the trees and danced with the sea.
Kites were laughing in colors so bright,
Who knew air could be such a comedic delight?

A surfboard slipped on the beach with flair,
The boardwalk's antics had me gasping for air.
As tumbleweeds rolled like old film stars,
The whole atmosphere twinkled with laughter from Mars.

So toss in your worries, let giggles ignite,
With windswept humor, the world feels just right.
Sing to the ocean, let your soul run free,
In the breezy embrace of good company!

Waves of Wonderment

A wave rolled over with a grand 'hello',
Tickling toes like a ticklish echo.
The ocean's tricks brought a wink to my eye,
As I splashed back and let out a joyful cry.

Strange sea creatures did a tap dance parade,
While dolphins jumped through a sunbeam cascade.
A crab in a hat blew a raspberry loud,
As I cheered on this wacky, merry crowd.

The foam made faces, a frothy delight,
Laughing and waving in the soft moonlight.
Seashells giggled with stories to share,
Whispering secrets in the salty air.

So come ride the waves, take a silly dive,
Where laughter bubbles, and all feel alive.
In this wavy wonder, let spirits roam,
In the arms of the ocean, you'll find a home!

Luminous Lagoon Tales

In a lagoon where the lights twinkle bright,
Frogs croaked jokes under the pale moonlight.
The dragonflies wore tiny bow ties and hats,
As they danced to tunes played by rascally rats.

The water glowed like a disco ball,
As fish swam up to join the call.
A splash from behind made everyone squeal,
"Oh there's nothing like this, it's surreal!"

With luminescent laughter, the night wore a grin,
While fireflies buzzed like a band from within.
The seaweed made jokes, and we all agreed,
This luminous party was exactly what we need.

As the night faded into dawn's gentle sweep,
We promised to keep all the memories deep.
In this joyful lagoon, with its magical light,
We found endless stories that felt just right!

The Tapestry of Tidal Songs

Waves dance in a slippery jig,
Seagulls swoop like a ladybug.
Crabs tap their feet in the sand,
As shells wear hats, oh how grand!

Frogs in the lagoon sing a tune,
Throwing a party beneath the moon.
Fish wear bow ties, looking so fine,
While mermaids sip coconut wine.

The breeze brings laughter, a playful breeze,
Tickling the trees like childhood tease.
Conch shells trumpet in silly parade,
As sandcastles proudly invade!

A pelican's dive is a splashy delight,
As dolphins compete in their own silly fight.
The beach is a stage, let the fun unfold,
Where every silly tale will be told!

Elysian Echoes on the Seashore

In the surf, a clam sings soft notes,
Synchronized with silly goats.
The tide pulls them closer, what a sight,
As they dance like stars in the night.

Palm trees sway, forget the stress,
Fronds make hats, in a fashion mess.
Marshmallow clouds float in blissful sway,
While children giggle and jump in play.

Seashells gossip, they chat and roar,
Sharing secrets from the ocean floor.
A coconut bids everyone adieu,
Rolling away, oh what a view!

The sun sets low, painting all bright,
As sand dollars shimmer, a funny sight.
Each wave whispers tales of mirth,
Giggles ride high, in the sand they birth!

The Poetry of Vista and Vastness

The sun giggles as it dips low,
Tickling the sea with a warm glow.
Seashells wear silly sunglasses tight,
While the dolphins put on a splashy flight.

Waves wiggle and sparkle, a cheeky grin,
As crickets join in, where to begin?
A toucan paints with its beak so bright,
Creating laughter in the fading light.

Kites fly high, like thoughts set free,
While a sandman plays on the beach with glee.
The sun whispers secrets, oh what a tease,
As everyone twirls in the warm breeze!

The horizon waves, in a playful jest,
Chasing shadows, never a rest.
In this canvas of fun, we all belong,
Each moment a note in this silly song!

Cradle of Coastal Echoes

Seagulls dive and squawk, they play,
Crabs are dancing, come what may.
Flip-flops slapping on the sand,
Shells are treasures, that's the plan.

Coconuts roll like silly dreams,
Tides come in with giggles and screams.
Sunshine tickles, feet are bare,
Relaxation fills the air.

Sandy castles rise and fall,
Water fights and laughter call.
Mermaids splash, a lopsided grin,
Chasing waves, let the fun begin!

At dusk, a party in the sky,
Fireflies twinkle, oh my, oh my!
Rhythms beat in hearts so wide,
In this cradle, joy won't hide.

Sunlit Soliloquy

Sunny rays tickle my toes,
Jellyfish dance like sassy prose.
Waves leap high in playful plays,
As the sun spills golden rays.

Beach balls bouncing, laughter's song,
Sharks in jokes, where they don't belong.
Ice cream drips and colors run,
Sticky fingers having fun.

Surfboards wobble, who'll take a fall?
Sand in sandwiches, oh, what a call!
Sunscreen battles, slather and swirl,
Hats flying off as we twirl.

No serious thoughts, just silly scenes,
Life's a beach—where nothing's routine!
Each splash is a giggle, a glint in the eye,
Under this sun, we dance and fly.

Swaying Palms and Whispering Waves

Palms wave like they're in a dance,
Even the breeze seems to prance.
Chill in a hammock, time's on hold,
Stories crackle, laughter bold.

Sandcastles with moats come alive,
Kites in the air like grand drives.
Seashells gossip, waves reply,
Seagulls laugh; they soar on by.

Lemonade sips; a sun-kissed cheer,
Fish-watching, and we draw near.
Bouncing seashells, all aglow,
Sprinkles and sunshine, what a show!

An ocean's hug, a salty kiss,
In this fun, what's not to miss?
Under bright skies, the world gets lighter,
With each wave, our hearts feel brighter.

Heartbeats of the Tide

Tides giggle, shift, and sway,
Pulling us in to dance and play.
Splashing feet in ocean's arms,
Chasing foam, enchanted charms.

Footprints sketching stories here,
In sandy scripts, there's nothing to fear.
Ahoy, matey! Let's set sail,
For treasure maps and funny tales.

Starfish nod and cheer us on,
As the sun dips low, the day's not gone.
With laughter light, we find our vibes,
Riding waves, we're catching tribes.

Each heartbeat in sync with the tide,
Fun is here, let's take a ride!
Life's a carnival, come join the dance,
In the rhythm of fun, we'll take our chance.

Dances of the Dusk Tide

As the sun dips low, crabs give a show,
Shuffling their feet, in the sand they flow.
Stars peek out bright, with a twinkling grin,
Fish gossiping tales, let the fun begin.

Turtles in caps, wearing shades, oh so cool,
Join in the jig, it's a nautical school.
With shells as their drums, they pound out the beat,
The ocean joins in, moving to their feet.

Seagulls squawk laughs, hovering from above,
Watching each move, oh how they do love.
The waves clap in rhythm, a splashy refrain,
Dance under the twilight, forget all your pain.

So come take a twirl on this sandy dance floor,
Where the laughter of creatures is hard to ignore.
With joy in our hearts and sand in our toes,
Each dusk is a party, that nobody knows.

Cadence of the Untamed Shore

On the wild beach, with a twist and a turn,
The seaweed waltz makes the young ones yearn.
Starfish in boots do the hokey pokey,
While otters perform, never feeling brokey.

With a flip and a flop, a clam takes the lead,
Leading the dance, fulfilling a need.
Crashing waves cheer, with their bubbly delight,
As the moon grins wide, cranking up the night.

Sea cucumbers sway, in their own groovy way,
While gulls break out into a loud cabaret.
The wind plays the flute, so thin and so sweet,
We shimmy and shake, to the rhythm's heartbeat.

So grab a new friend and spin 'round with glee,
In this wacky parade, we all dance for free.
On the untamed shore, life's a whimsical game,
Where laughter and music make everything tame.

Solitude's Sweet Cadence

In the quiet of dusk, all alone on a rock,
I try to tap dance, but just hear a cluck.
The crabs roll their eyes, calling me quite lame,
Yet I keep on trying, for fun is the aim.

I start a conga, oh what a delight,
Bubbles from fish splash, they join in the fight.
Seashells are clapping, oh what a surprise,
As the dolphins pop up, with glimmering eyes.

The sea breeze chuckles, giving waves a good nudge,
Making me giggle, I won't budge.
Each flip of a fin, brings a glimmer of wit,
In solitude's joy, I refuse to quit.

So I'll dance on this rock until the sun bows low,
With the ocean as partner, we steal the show.
Solitude's sweet, with a twist and a spin,
A funny old dance, where the joy begins.

Nautical Nocturne

The stars are my band, in the night's cool embrace,
As I shimmy and swirl in a clumsy old race.
Whales hum a tune, deep down in the blue,
While jellyfish flash like a disco anew.

Octopus offers a funky high five,
With each twist and turn, I feel so alive.
The plankton join in for a flickering show,
In this underwater rave, we all steal the flow.

The seafoam jives, in a topsy-turvy whirl,
While squids twirl around in a slimy swirled pearl.
Even starfish giggle, each on their own beat,
In this quirky ballet, it's hard to stay neat.

So dance under starlight, let laughter ignite,
With the ocean as witness, it's pure delight.
Nautical vibes with a twist and a quirk,
As the rhythm takes hold, and we all go berserk.

Sapphire Spells of Evening's Tide

The sun dips low, a cheeky grin,
Fish put on shades, let the fun begin.
Crabs dance sideways, a wiggly sight,
While dolphins giggle, oh what a night!

Stars blink down like winking lights,
The breeze, it teases, and feels just right.
Seashells joke, 'We're all plays on the sand!'
As jellyfish sway, like they've got a band!

Laughter bubbles in every wave,
Sandcastles bow, so bold and brave.
The moon's on stage, and what a show!
With coconuts clapping, go, go, go!

Gulls take turns to tell silly tales,
Of treasure maps and fishy scales.
Under the stars, the night spins fast,
In sapphire spells, the fun will last!

The Songbird's Call at Dusk

A parrot squawks, in full delight,
'The worms are dancing, come join tonight!'
Toucans toss jokes with flair and style,
As crickets chirp, 'Stay here a while!'

Over the pond, frogs leap with cheer,
Croaking in chorus—what a scene here!
With fireflies blinking, making a fuss,
Nature's comedy, on a grand bus!

With each sunrise, the chuckles renew,
As fish pop up, and say, 'Boo-hoo!'
The trees sway gently, still swaying on,
By the end of dusk, all worries are gone!

In this realm, laughter's the guide,
So bring your giggles, come take a ride.
The songbirds sing, in goofy delight,
As twilight unfolds, oh what a night!

The Mosaic of Aquatic Melodies

Goldfish float, like bubbles of glee,
In a sea of tiles, oh so free!
Octopus plays piano, eight hands a-blast,
While starfish jam, it's a party cast!

Coral reefs cheer with colors bright,
They wiggle and giggle, what a sight!
Underneath waves where secrets hide,
Laughter erupts, like an oceanic tide!

A seahorse spins, in a groovy trap,
Singing along with a perky clap.
Turtles race, but move like a crawl,
In this aquatic world, they have a ball!

As bubbles rise, the fun interweaves,
Where jellyfish dance, and nothing deceives.
In this mosaic of jokes and cheer,
The ocean's tune, is crystal clear!

Rhapsody of the Winding Bay

Sailboats zigzag with playful flair,
While seagulls argue, none seem to care.
A parasol spins, in the warm balmy breeze,
As waves come in, just like a tease!

Sand between toes, nothing feels wrong,
As children giggle, to their own song.
Pineapple drinks with tiny umbrellas,
Dancing on tables, these fruity fella's!

A crab in a costume, a sight to behold,
Prancing about, oh so bold!
The sunset paints colors, the sky like a flame,
In this winding bay, it's all just a game.

With laughter and echoes of joyous glee,
The night wraps up, oh so carefree.
In rhapsody here, where spirits soar,
The memory lingers, forevermore!

Lullaby of the Seashell Shore

The waves chat softly at dusk's door,
While crabs dance a jig, asking for more.
Seashells giggle as they play on the sand,
Caught in the tide's ticklish hand.

Starfish wear hats, oh what a sight!
Clams clap along, no worries tonight.
Pelicans dive, then waddle away,
As laughter echoes, come join the fray.

The tide brings secrets from afar,
Shells glisten bright like a tiny star.
A conch shells out tunes of delight,
While sand dunes nod in this playful night.

Under the moon, all creatures conspire,
To frolic and jig like they're in a choir.
With each splash, a chuckle is cast,
On this shore, where joy holds fast.

Swaying in Paradise

Palm trees sway in a merry old dance,
While the sun's warm rays give joy a chance.
Coconuts giggle, it's quite the scene,
As parrots squawk jokes like they're on a screen.

Flip-flops flop with each playful stride,
Bikini-clad folks with laughter wide.
Tropical smoothies whirling in bliss,
Who knew the fun could taste like this?

Beach towels flutter like flags in a race,
Seagulls squawk jokes, just keeping pace.
Sandcastles wobble, the tide waits to tickle,
As folks gather round for a good old giggle.

With sunsets splashed in orange and pink,
Happiness flows, who needs to think?
Every wave whispers, "Let's joke some more,"
In this joyful land, who could ask for more?

Mosaic of the Coral Canvas

Beneath the waves, colors collide,
Fish swim in pairs, like a wild joyride.
Coral winks, showing off its hues,
Tickling the gills of gossiping blues.

Turtles dabble in bubbles of glee,
Jellyfish jiggle, come dance with me!
Anemones giggle in sway with the tide,
Making new friends in this ocean wide.

Seahorses twirl in their quirky spree,
While clownfish cavort, oh so carefree.
Starry-eyed dreams drift on the waves,
As laughter echoes in watery caves.

The drums of the deep play taps and tones,
Seaweed sways to the rhythmic moans.
Each splash and bubble sings out a tune,
Under the watch of the silvery moon.

The Pulse of Quietude

In the quiet nooks where the breeze tells tales,
Chill vibes flow while the seaweed flails.
Breezes whisper as turtles roam,
Each splash sounds like a sneaky home.

Ocean's pulse beats, a gentle thrum,
Fish giggle softly as they come.
Drifting in calm, the laughter swells,
In a dance of mischief, where mystery dwells.

The crab pulls pranks with a sly little grin,
Jellyfish waltz with a shimmering spin.
Starfish play hide-and-seek with the sun,
In this quiet land, there's always fun.

Whales hum tunes that echo far,
Crashing waves join in, a wild bazaar.
Even the rocks wear silly hats,
In this serene spot where humor chats.

Rhythms of the Coral Cauldron

Underwater dancing fish do sway,
While crabs wear hats and shout hooray!
Turtles glide with a goofy grin,
In the cauldron's beat, all join in.

Jellyfish jiggle, a sight to see,
As sea horses ride on a rolling spree.
Octopuses juggle seashells with glee,
In this coral dance, we all agree!

Starfish spin like tops that whirl,
While clams do pirouettes in a swirl.
The kelp grows wild, a tangled twirl,
As waves applaud this ocean girl!

So join the fun, don't be uptight,
Let's make some laughter last all night.
In the coral cauldron, all take flight,
With silly moves, our hearts feel light!

Tidal Whispers in the Twilight

As the sun dips low, the tides do tease,
Fish tell secrets with the greatest ease.
Crickets chirp in rhythm so sweet,
While gentle waves dance to a funky beat.

Seagulls squawk in a melodic way,
As mermaids giggle, at play all day.
The lighthouse winks, a cheeky peer,
While shells pass whispers for all to hear.

Moonbeams shimmy on the water's face,
Tide pools reflect a hilarious place.
Starfish hold hands, a silly sight,
In twilight's embrace, all feels just right!

So, laugh with the ocean, let spirits rise,
In the playful aura, let joy be the prize.
With laughter and tides mixed in a dance,
Every wave and whisper brings a chance!

Vibrations of the Celestial Seas

Cosmic waves ripple with a flair,
As dolphins perform in the cosmic air.
Planets hum while the seashells groove,
In this grand show, all feel the move.

Starry night casts a quirky glow,
As fish pop popcorn from below.
Comets dash across the deep,
While crabs hold a dance-off, what a leap!

The moon plays drums as waves do clap,
With shooting stars that go kabap!
Every splash is a cosmic cheer,
In these celestial seas, no need for fear!

So let's sway like the ocean's embrace,
Join the feast in this stellar place.
With laughter and music, we'll make our mark,
As vibrations spark joy 'til it's dark!

Footprints in the Sugar Sand

Sandy footprints lead the way,
Little crabs giggle on their foray.
Seagulls squawk, 'Watch where you tread!'
In this sugar land, let fun be spread!

Waves race in with a bubbly laugh,
Carrying shells as a quirky staff.
Each footprint tells a story of glee,
In the dampened sand, we dance carefree.

Beach balls bounce with laughter's sound,
As little tots tumble all around.
Sunshades wave like flags on display,
In the sugar sand, we frolic and play!

So let's leave prints, make memories bright,
Splashing in joy from morning till night.
With every grain and giggle, let's cheer,
The footprints we leave will always near!

Ghost Notes from the Forgotten Isles

In the distance, a parrot squawks,
Telling tales of old, funny mocks.
Crabs dance on the beach, all in sync,
While the coconut falls, and I just wink.

A ghostly tune fills the salty air,
Mischief lingers, everywhere!
Jellyfish jiggle, in silly delight,
Underneath the moon, oh what a sight!

Waves whisper secrets to the sand,
A laughter echoes from the land.
Shells giggle, as they roll and play,
On this forgotten, jolly bay.

With each splash, a chuckle is heard,
An orchestra of fun, not a single word.
So come join the merry, breezy dance,
In this strange world, give joy a chance!

Threads of Paradise in the Wind

A kite flies high, tangled in trees,
Caught in a story told by the breeze.
Palm fronds wave, with a cheeky grin,
As the sun dips low, let the fun begin!

Bananas in hats, dancing on the shore,
Each fruit a jester, begging for more.
Flip-flops chatter, letting sly jokes,
While seagulls squawk in silly strokes.

Laughter ebbs and flows, like the tide,
Chasing seaweed, our silly guide.
We spin on the sand, feet barely touching,
With every twirl, the joy is clenching.

As twilight falls, the stars begin to hum,
And even the crabs can't resist the fun.
In this paradise, laughter flies,
With threads of delight that never die.

Undercurrents of the Celestial Sea

Bubbles whisper secrets, under the waves,
Fish wearing hats, oh what brave knaves!
A dolphin giggles as he leaps high,
While octopuses juggle, oh my, oh my!

A treasure map drawn on a seashell's face,
Leading us to this fun-filled place.
Crabby conspiracies and fishy fun,
What shall we do when the day is done?

With every splash and wink of the eye,
The sea's got humor that won't run dry.
Shells roll around, like they own the floor,
Cheering each other for that extra score.

The moon's a clown, painting the sea,
With glittery beams, so carelessly.
Join in the laughter, let your soul be free,
In these currents of joy, forever we'll be.

Dreamscapes in the Shimmering Bay

A floaty jelly drifts by with grace,
Blowing bubbles as if in a race.
Seashells gossip, sharing their tales,
Along with the crabs, who drive tiny trails.

In the shimmering bay, we twirl and sway,
Fish put on capes to show us the way.
Starfish are judges, as we break out moves,
A dance-off ensues, everybody grooves!

The breeze carries whispers of nighttime's giggle,
As the boat anchored writes a cheeky riddle.
Moonbeams tinkle, casting glittery glee,
While we prance about, wild and carefree.

So join the hilarity, slip on your shoes,
In the dreamscapes, there's nothing to lose.
We'll laugh with the waves, till night turns to dawn,
The fun never fades; it just carries on!

The Language of Pelagic Breezes

The seagulls squawk in a silly song,
While crabs dance wildly, it won't be long.
The tides keep whispering jokes so bright,
As fish in the waves giggle with delight.

A pirate's hat floats, a treasure's near,
But it's just more pizza! Oh dear, oh dear!
A dolphin grins, wearing shades so cool,
While starfish pose at the sandy school.

There's laughter echoing under the sun,
With sea cucumbers ready for fun.
Breezy surprises float by like dreams,
Where even the clams burst out with beams.

With rhythms that sway like a clown on a spree,
The ocean's a stage, just look and you'll see!
It's a dance of the waves, and oh what a sight,
Where every soft splash brings joy to the night.

Whims of the Coastal Twilight

As the sun dips low, crabs start to prance,
While starry fish seem to join in the dance.
The moon's a big cookie, floating so wide,
And turtles hold parties, oh what a ride!

Seaweed wiggles, like it's got some flair,
With the jellyfish twirling, spinning in air.
A walrus wearing a blingy gold chain,
Sings tunes to the stars, oh what a refrain!

Seashells gossip like friends at the shore,
As laughter erupts, who could ask for more?
The breeze tells secrets, and the waves retort,
While sandcastles cheer, holding a court.

With each crashing wave, comes a ticklish cheer,
Whims of the twilight, brought close and near.
In this quirky world where laughter is found,
The coast is alive with tickles abound.

Dreaming in the Shade of Palms

A coconut drops with a thud and a laugh,
While monkeys concoct a most silly craft.
Under the palms, all the creatures unite,
For stories of mischief that dance in the light.

A parrot insists it can dance like a pro,
While crabs roll their eyes, saying, 'Oh no!'
The breeze tickles noses, what a delight!
As dolphins splash tales of their daring flights.

Under the sun's watch, the laughter runs high,
With shells and some sand as our confetti sky.
Rusty old flip-flops join in the parade,
As flip-flopping fish twirl, oh how they've played!

In dreams of the shade, the stories take flight,
With giggles and wiggles, they glow in the night.
So let's all remember this fun-loving band,
Where laughter and sunshine go hand in hand.

Melodies of the Pristine Waters

Bubbles are popping like tunes in the air,
As fish play their trumpets without any care.
A sea turtle strums on a driftwood guitar,
While the octopus juggles with shells from afar.

The rhythm of splashes is joined by a whale,
Who hums silly words to a comical tale.
Each wave sings a note, as the gulls join in,
Making melodies swift, full of laughter and spin.

Fiddler crabs boast of their moves on the sand,
While clams clap their shells at the jiving band.
The currents dance lightly, twirling with grace,
As fish share their jokes with a wink and a chase.

Under the stars, where the waters are wide,
The moon hums along, with a sparkle and glide.
In these pristine waters, let's join the jest,
For laughter is music, and life is the best.

Tides That Shape the Shoreline

The waves crash down with a silly splash,
They tickle my toes and cause a dash.
Fish in a frenzy, they dance with glee,
Making my troubles swim far from me.

The sun's a joker, it plays peek-a-boo,
While crabs in the sand do the limbo too.
Seagulls squawk jokes as they swoop and dive,
We're all part of this beachy jive.

A starfish winks with a goofy grin,
As children giggle, let the fun begin.
Shells chatting loudly in their own dialect,
They gossip about all the waves they wreck.

So let's grab a drink, a coconut cheer,
With laughter and sunshine, there's nothing to fear.
The tides keep rolling, they never tire,
In laughter, we find our hearts' own choir.

Lullabies of the Lost Archipelago

In hammock's sway, I hear a tune,
From wise old dolphins under the moon.
They sing of treasures and shipwrecks bold,
While groovy seagrass shakes like gold.

The stars twinkle like giggling friends,
Matching the rhythm that never ends.
A parrot screeches a comedic line,
As fish perform a synchronized dine.

With crickets chirping their offbeat song,
And waves dancing wildly, it all feels wrong.
But laughter echoes through this strange bliss,
A funny paradise that's hard to miss.

Here's to the nights wrapped in a light breeze,
Where every funny moment puts me at ease.
We sway and laugh till the dawn's bright light,
In lullabies crafted of pure delight.

Currents in a Coral Dream

Coral castles with a wink and a nudge,
Some sea turtles join in, they never judge.
An octopus juggles his shimmering stones,
While fish in bow ties address the drones.

The currents swirl like a grand parade,
With silly seaweed that's never afraid.
We spin and whir, in this underwater fest,
As dolphins perform their favourite jest.

A clam makes a joke, but it's hard to hear,
With bubbles bursting and cheer everywhere.
Laughter rolls in like the waves on the shore,
In this coral dream, who could ask for more?

So float on a wave of humor and cheer,
And let the ocean tickle your ear.
For in this realm where the funny reigns,
Our silly hearts swim without any chains.

Song of the Saltwater Serenade

In salty air, where silliness breeds,
The gulls tell tales of whimsical deeds.
A crab in a tux, all ready to dance,
With every wave comes a new chance.

The buoy's a joker, keeps bobbing around,
While seaweed giggles, unbound by the sound.
The tide hums a melody, soft and light,
As sunlight sparkles, oh what a sight!

Mermaids chuckling, with shells on their hats,
Invite us to join in their aquatic chats.
With each splash, a punchline flips out of view,
Making our hearts sing a tune fresh and new.

So let's join the frolic, let worries aplenty,
Float on the waves and stay oh so merry.
In this salty serenade, laughter is key,
Where joy is the treasure, wild and free.

Chasing the Coastal Song

On the shore, the seagulls squawk,
Dancing crab does the waddle walk.
A starfish grins, a silly sight,
While clams play peek-a-boo all night.

The ocean hums a playful tune,
Shells join in, like a raucous croon.
Frogs in frolicking boots do leap,
While fishy friends just snore and sleep.

A sandy dog struts his fancy flair,
Finding treasures beyond compare.
With each wave, funny shapes appear,
Laughter bubbles up from here to there.

The tide sweeps in, with a blushing grin,
A jellyfish jig, as the fun begins.
So grab your friends, come join the glee,
In this zany world, so wild and free.

Ballad of the Twilight Waters

The sun dips low, a cheeky tease,
Mermaids sing to the frosty breeze.
A dolphin flips, with a wink or two,
Sharing secrets with the stars anew.

A crab in boots starts a one-man show,
While octopuses play limbo below.
The seaweed sways, with a giggle and twirl,
As the shimmering waves begin to whirl.

A turtle's hat flies high and proud,
As pelicans gather, drawing a crowd.
With a splash and a laugh, they join the fun,
As twilight blankets everyone.

So toast with shells, let happiness flow,
In twilight waters where laughter grows.
With each silly creature, a tale will start,
A whimsical boat ride in every heart.

Driftwood Dreams

The driftwood really knows how to glide,
Carrying secrets from the ocean wide.
It hums a tune from the days of yore,
As crabs hold hands and fish dance on the shore.

A bearded barnacle joins the chase,
While snappy clams race, just keep up the pace!
On a wave high, a starfish spins,
With each little splash, the laughter begins.

Sea-horses wearing shiny crowns,
Gather to chant silly ocean sounds.
A hermit crab dons a flashy suit,
While fish throw confetti, what a hoot!

The sun drips gold, it's time to play,
In driftwood dreams, we'll laugh away.
With goofy waves crashing on the scene,
Every moment, a quirkier dream.

Rhythm of the Lapping Waves

The lapping waves sing a silly tune,
While fish do the cha-cha under the moon.
A clownfish juggles, with shells for flair,
As a dolphin dons a bright pink pair.

The sea foam giggles, sprinkles like gold,
Each ripple dances, a sight to behold.
In the warm sand, footprints twist and glide,
A crab's salsa moves get us all fired.

The tide rolls in, with a splashy clap,
Seashells cheer, in their colorful caps.
A starry night, full of silly flights,
Where laughter echoes in playful sights.

So let's wade in, with grins and cheers,
In this rhythm of fun, we'll shed all fears.
With every wave, we dance and sway,
In the heart of this frolicsome display.

www.ingramcontent.com/pod-product-compliance
Lightning Source LLC
Chambersburg PA
CBHW072135070526
44585CB00016B/1690